THIN KIMONO

THIN KIMONO

MICHAEL EARL CRAIG

WAVE BOOKS

SEATTLE AND

NEW YORK

Published by Wave Books

www.wavepoetry.com

Wave Books titles are distributed to the trade by

Consortium Book Sales and Distribution

Phone: 800-283-3572 / SAN 631-760X

This title is available in limited edition hardcover

directly from the publisher

Library of Congress Cataloging-in-Publication Data

Craig, Michael Earl.

Thin kimono / Michael Earl Craig.—1st ed.

p. cm.

ISBN 978-1-933517-46-9 (pbk. : alk. paper)

I. Title.

PS3603.R3553T47 2010

811'.6—dc22

2010005789

Designed and composed by Quemadura

Printed in the United States of America

9 8 7 6 5 4 3 2

First Edition

Wave Books 023

FOR SUSAN

CONTENTS

II

III

In a hall of the Louvre, a child cries in terror

at the sight of another child's portrait.

CESAR VALLEJO

THIN KIMONO

DO NOT DISTURB

Now if you'll come down this hallway—mind the cobwebs—
we'll pop out here into this sunny, walled-in courtyard,
almost entirely choked front-to-back with rampant ivy.
The vines are waist high and cover the birdbath, a defunct fountain,
a gas grill and some garden gnomes.
Near the center is a white plastic table, the top of which
can just barely be seen. Slight lumps in the deep ivy indicate
where a few chairs are, positioned around the table.
Propped up in one of these chairs is a dead man.
In front of him is an old Underwood typewriter
with a sheet of blank paper fed into it.
Beside the typewriter is a box of Kleenex.
We will be careful not to disturb this man, as he is working
on something very important. You might be inclined
to lean in with your pencil here, to add a few lines
in an effort to elaborate on this scenario, or on this man's
situation. But I assure you that is wholly unnecessary.

I

I'M COMING OVER TO SEE YOU

It's a gorgeous day.
You can't make a record if
you ain't got nothing to say.

Bending over and
grabbing your ankles at
the crosswalk can
seem a little forward.

Years pass and
I can't forget Cape Cod—

smell of sunscreen,
steak house,
Taffy Towne;

the bloodshot eyes of
the Dutch nanny,
a bourbon in one hand,
gin gimlet in the other;

when it was time to leave,
the old lobster with one
claw climbed quietly
into our rental car—

all the while knowing I
must concentrate, *focus*,
stay in the moment for a second.

The plane is taking off.
I have fastened my seat belt.
I am coming to see you . . .

Charles the seeing-eye dog wears a blue raincoat.
The stewardess writes her eyebrows on with pencil.
Mom always called me "enthusiastic"
when I'd pull my underwear on too hard
and rip them to my chin.

Baby rabbits in your yard.
When I knock don't let me in.

BLUEBIRDS

I'm sitting in my brown chair.
I have dirt under each of my fingernails.
Except for the pinkies.

I remember hearing of
the gorgeous town blonde
who told reporters
she'd never date a man with
dirt under his nails.

It's a poet's job
to be dragged by an ankle
through town.

A poem shouldn't require
a lot of book learning
to understand, I once wrote,
and Tina leaned

over my desk and said,
To understand what?
I didn't say anything.

Trying again I wrote
in capital letters THE READER
CAN ALMOST BE DUMB REALLY
AND STILL GET MY POEMS.
Tina nodded her head.

The ankle caught up
in the stirrup of a galloping
horse.

I slump over in my chair.
It's like I'm covered in bluebirds.
Little brilliant ones.

And when I say this,
"little brilliant ones,"
I lisp a little like a man
who's been punched hard in the mouth
but still wants to talk bluebirds.

THE BAD CLOWN

I was at the acupuncturist's.
It was my first time.
She put the needles in as I told jokes
to the ceiling. She put more needles in.
I tensed up and let out a demented clown laugh.
It made her stop for a second.
There was a gentle gong-and-bell track
piped in via hidden speakers.
"The speakers are in the jade plant," she said.
I tensed up again. I was golden brown.
I felt like one of those bad clowns.
The kind that hide in the sewers.
The acupuncturist was trying to help me.

THE SORENSEN EFFECT

Sorensen was a professor of philosophy,
the author of thirty-two books and hundreds
of published articles and critical reviews,
a bachelor, twice nominated for a Nobel Prize,
and the recipient of countless other awards
in both philosophy and the humanities.

Sorensen lived like an outcast
with his exceptionally thick, white beard,
which many felt housed both his brain and his soul.
When you looked at Sorensen it was this beard
that you saw. Later you'd find yourself incapable
of describing his face or his voice.
This beard was always dusty and often had
some oatmeal or a strip of bacon in it.

One day Sorensen had a surprise visitor,
a young woman who had traveled a great distance
to meet her hero after eight months
of unreturned letters and phone calls.
Sorensen was almost blind. His place was a wreck—

dishes in the sink, a filthy tub and toilet, stacks of books
and yellowed magazines blocking hallways
and completely overtaking the screened-in porch.

Sorensen was oblivious.
He asked this young woman to finely chop
a three-pound bag of almonds.
The young woman, it turned out, was very good at this.
Despite his terrible eyesight Sorensen
could safely say he'd never seen such
a neat and rapidly growing pile,
at which point he asked the young woman
to remove his beard—to please shave his beard
completely off. The young woman stopped chopping.
She wiped her hands on a dirty towel and began
collecting her things, her coat and her backpack.
She was shocked and a little scared.
But Sorensen was somehow able to convince her
not only to stay—to put down her coat and bag—
but to carry out his wishes, and in no time at all
he had seated himself in a chair before the young woman.

As Sorensen joked and chatted amiably, the young woman
used electric sheep clippers from beneath the sink
and in a fairly steady hand she made ten or eleven
downward passes, the clippers vibrating confidently,

and soon the beard lay in ruin all about Sorensen's lap and feet.
He looked like a plucked chicken. He looked suddenly cold
and smaller, and a little younger. His eyes looked milky
in the late afternoon light. He sat as if tied to the chair.
He was ready for some ice cream.

Over thirty years have passed and this woman
has never recovered from shaving Sorensen.
They'd eaten some ice cream and parted company politely.
Sorensen was found years later, dead in his garden,
a smile on his face just beneath a carefully waxed handlebar mustache.
But by that time the young woman had completely lost track
of Sorensen's activities, as well as those of friends and family.
Soon she was incapable of making a salad
or combing her hair. She has been sitting in this chair
[*camera moves in on the woman*]
beside this window for at least a decade now.
[*oboe & clarinet…*]
It is a strange and wondrous world we live in.
But this is no time for platitudes.

WHEN IT'S TIME

When it's time I'd like to be buried
in a simple wooden coffin.
A pine-board box.
Or even a thick, waxed cardboard box.
Hell, it doesn't even need to be thick.
Or waxed. See what you think.

And drop me in there any old way,
in any man's clothes,
but be sure to tip my head back
and prop my jaw wide open
and get my arms up in front of me
like I'm playing the piano.

Whether or not they sew my eyelids shut
doesn't matter. But don't comb my hair.
And don't play the drums.

When it's time I'd like to have everyone be quiet.
People can dance if they want
but I do ask for absolute silence.
I know I'll be dead but

I don't want there to be even the sound
of a pin dropping.

I'll be in my box looking up.
My arms will suggest a gentle concerto.
Or maybe a ragtime number.
And it shouldn't be seen as a look of horror on my face,
for I've had a good time in this body.

So when it's time and people
have gathered around my cardboard box,
or whatever you've chosen,
to look down at me in silence,
their feet shuffling soundlessly in place,
the madhouse rhythms coursing through them,
their hair whipping in the gale-force wind,
their cheeks vibrating like Jell-O
as if the earth were about to explode,
and no pins are dropping—do you hear me?—
it is *silent*—

I will then be the charred center
of an enormous yellow flower,
which will be very confusing for some,
and somewhat embarrassing for me,
but I'll be dead, and so won't notice.

TODAY, FOR EXAMPLE

Every now and then I wonder if I fucked up with this horseshoeing thing, but then I talk with friends in academia and, well, I'm okay with my choices. Take today for example. I worked on Tom (old, crippled, needs therapeutic shoes), Jimmy (unsure about the world, collapses violently when he hears loud noises, likes to cut himself), and Puck (from Philadelphia, lanky, neurotic, tried to pull the hitch rail over, was wearing a red spandex fly mask). They were all covered in mud and fecal matter. I listened to the radio some. It was raining in the mountains.

I WAS THINKING

1

I thought: *It's Wednesday, I'm*
gonna get me a belt buckle with
a bald eagle on it.
The wind chimes went batty.

Later the wrestling coach spat
a wet flake of his Swisher Sweet
at the dashboard, which
came off his tongue wrong
and hit me in the cheek.

I thought: *Coach's eyes are like farm animals.*
And: *all the paths I could take*
through the garden if I were a vapor . . .

Suddenly it was time.
A single black llama ran briskly up a hill.
There was pinochle in another town.
The hungry actress ordered sea bass.
And somehow from my poem came your feeling of consent.

While slicing olives I remembered Richard Nixon:
"When the President does it,
that means that it is not illegal."
I thought about this.

And then Ronald Reagan:
"Government is like a big baby—
an alimentary canal with
a big appetite at one end
and no responsibility at the other."
I could really picture it.

And Albert Einstein:
"Something deeply hidden had to be behind things."
I sliced another olive.

As this olive rocked open, into halves,
I felt a kind of roadside flare go off in my head:

"It is a human right to be a coward."
JOHAN JÖNSON

The flare sputtered. It was wet:

"So you, too, like fruitcake?"

ROBERT WALSER, UPON MEETING LENIN

IN ZURICH, DURING THE WAR

I sat back.
I had grown tired of slicing olives.

3

When PETA tried to crucify Werner Herzog
for lashing a monkey to a cross
(*Even Dwarfs Started Small*)
Herzog said: "We only had that monkey
on the cross for sixty seconds."

Now this was more like it.
Somehow this explained everything.

The actress had gently wolfed her sea bass.
Wednesday was passing quietly like a very loose cannon.

NIGHT VISIT

I'm awakened at 3 a.m. to the sound of an owl.
It takes me a minute to find my glasses.
I press my face to the window.
A silver flash crosses the yard.
It settles into an owl shape on a nearby post.
My nose and eyes are stinging.
A stinging behind my face.
Like some kind of problem behind a billboard.
Why would a man look at an owl and start to cry?
My body is trying to reject something.
I have no idea what that is.
The owl is sitting in the moonlight.
The yard is completely still.

THIS I BELIEVE

I don't know how to behave but
I know what I believe. I believe
that if I stick my head in the oven
I won't take it out. I believe in
corduroy couch cushions. I believe
in digging a tunnel with a small
silver spoon. I believe in tunneling
with this spoon under the city
and never giving up.
I believe in after-breakfast naps
and Russian roulette—
Russian roulette while eating ice cream
as I watch the evening news.
I believe in the evening news.
And I believe in celebrity.

I believe in those photos
on the web of Putin playing doubles
Ping-Pong, outdoors, in his Speedo.
(Find those.) I believe in haircuts
and bubble gum, and putting my face

down into a pillow or cushion,
and that when I do this I will see
the future, plus other cultures, most
of them, and I'll get work done
that couldn't be done another way.

I believe in tacos and mortification.
I believe that all people fall
into one of two categories: Doonesbury or Far Side.
Well, or Andy Capp. Andy Capp type people.
They're everywhere.

HONESTLY

When it comes right down to it I'm a hopeless romantic.
And you, you are a scheming opportunistic leech.
And Chad is "the orphan." You follow me?

Or maybe I'm the leech, and Chad is still "the orphan,"
and you're the doe-eyed dreamer.

Laverne's the token Libertarian with the Mercury
Cougar, its trunk full of deer meat.

Stu is the pragmatist. The classic pragmatist.
With one foot in the grave and the other at the movies.
Or is it the other way around?

Donald is the quintessential blonde bombshell.

And here is where things for you take a turn for the worse.
You're out in a meadow. You have your head down.
You look like you're grazing on something.
Me? I just happen to be there.

I haven't felt hopeless in a long time.

Stu means well but can't help anyone.

Something in the way you have your head tilted . . .

I feel the cables tightening in me.

We won't return to Laverne.

Donald arrives. He lets his matted hair down

as one might dump out a tarp full of condoms.

And Chad. Well, well, well, let's take a closer look at Chad . . .

HE QUICKLY TOLD HIS LIFE STORY

A man was out backcountry skiing when he fell
and did something, broke something,
and he couldn't get up.

He lay there in the snow, miles from any road.
His dog was with him and as he lay there, this dog
raced about and snapped at the snow
and hopped over the man once, twice.
The man spoke to the dog but the dog did not recognize him.
Did not, the man sensed, seem to recognize him.

It was cold and getting dark.
The man could not feel his legs.
The dog was there, he barked insanely at a squirrel.
The man called the dog's name, ordered the dog to sit.
The man asked the dog to please come to him.

As darkness fell the man wondered if this was Death.
The dog was gone. The man lay on his back and cursed.
It was night.

Hours passed. The man thought he heard something.
The beam of a flashlight came stabbing at the trees.
It was his wife, she'd come upon him in the snow.
When he saw her he cried out. She knelt beside him
and he quickly recounted for her his life story,

starting with the birth canal, his first blankets—
then the sun, how it warmed the universe—
jobs he'd loved and hated—his golf clubs—his marriage—
a couple of cars he'd owned.
He blinked his eyes. He was angry.

The man raved but was alone. There was no one.
His limbs went out like candlewicks and he felt a flame
glowing in his chest. The dog ran like mad through the woods,
snapping at the wind.

VOTED BEST LEGS, CLASS OF '88

I'm lying in my motel room in the dark
listening to the muffled voices on another man's radio
coming through the wall near my head.
I'd held my Cobb salad at the airport like it was an infant,
and slept as if drugged from takeoff to touchdown,
dreaming I was a famous doctor tearing into a pastry
with an expensive laser, one monkey after another
off to organ-grinder school, tough broads in the Melissa
Etheridge vein, some everyday vitriol in a shaky hand,
Jesus tossing the various fishes into the crowd,
the Pope's niece's daughter running from us (we followed her),
and then like I said the plane touched down.
Now I'm here wearing my dark brown suit
and lying on the dark brown bedspread like Gulliver,
tied flat by the little people.

IT IS OCTOBER

It is October.
A bumblebee crawls into a crack
in the plank to die.

Still, I am here on the porch writing
a short story about tender young carrots.

The breeze would like to forget me,
the trees to step over me,
the grass to erase me.

A poem begins to arrive about
the best blurb writer in Europe.
A prizewinning blurb writer from Hamburg.

I set my pen down.

*

It's October.
The senator wore a large bowie knife on his belt.
It clanked once on the side of the toilet.

Folderol in diapers.
Badminton (the metaphor).
A preoccupation with salad.

After lunch a human head came out, on its own,
from behind the boathouse.
This was supposedly an omen
but we took it as an inconvenience.

Turns out ants were carrying it,
same as a hoagie.

*

It is October.

And Jan—
your goats are not dying.
They're actually in good shape.
Went carefully through the herd
and could find no problems.
I examined their feet,
combed them thoroughly for burs,
milked each with gusto,
wrestling only briefly with Barbara.

POEM WITH CRAB PUFF

At a crowded party on the Upper East Side—mostly intellectuals and artists, a few physicists, some Wall Street types and an oil tycoon—there was a potato farmer's widow from Idaho with whom basically no one wanted to speak. She stood somewhat cornered with a small plate in one hand, her other hand in the pocket of a light blue cardigan.

It started out casually enough: someone wanted to know what she thought about books, about theater, about music, about politics. She was very polite, she smiled, but had little to say. They made a few jokes at first. Then they became agitated, they accused her of being stingy with herself, and eventually of being an arrogant elitist.

She stepped back and set down her crab puff. A sense of doom washed over her like a long, low note on a tuba. "You are a traitor," someone said. She looked at them nervously. Then, "No, you are an idiot!" someone shouted. She cleared her throat. "I'd like to comment on your poached pears," she said, getting carefully down on her knees. They attacked her with their forks and saucers.

AT PRETZEL HUT

He is fat, shaved bald, kind looking.
He wears a coarse robe and sandals.
He is Buddha.

We're in line at the mall, at Pretzel Hut.
He's turned to me to ask for a nickel.
He works next door at Enlightened Lotions.

Buddha gets paid to mill around the mall
and hand out samples. His breath stinks
like an ashtray. Spring jasmine ashtray.

BUBBLES CAME FROM THEIR NOSES

He wasn't supposed to be there.
(This is how any number of poems begin.)
He had his goggles. And his nose plugs.

He was underwater, and pretending
to be fixing a ladder
bolted to the side of the pool.

The participants in
the synchronized swimming workshop
eyed him cautiously.
Each of them had her arms out
like Christ on the cross
and they hovered near the bottom,
but not *on* the bottom,
and this was what fascinated him.

Many of the swimmers had their palms
turned slightly up, their arms
bent a bit at the elbows,
and this gave them the appearance
of those carefully weighing something,

two things I suppose, perhaps pitting
one thing against another, but in a fair
and emotionless manner, and this
made them seem to him both judgmental
and blasé, which he liked.

There were over two dozen of them.
Their hands pendulated a little.
This trued them.
The colors of the pool
were deep blue and turquoise
with shafts of gold light in spots,
and the swimmers farthest from him
looked ghostly, like faded blueprints
of swimmers.

It was calm down there. Serene.
He heard an occasional dull clanking from
he didn't know where.

Bubbles came from the swimmers' noses.
They eyed him cautiously.

And then one of them, a chubby one, she
appeared to be the leader . . .
she made her move.

Her chest was forward, her shoulders back.
She was squinting. Her goggles were clear
and seemed part of her head.
She began to move out ahead of the group.
He sensed a slight buzz in the water.

She reminded him of a sea horse.
She was expressionless.
She moved as if she had a little motor behind her.
She came right at the man,
slowly, and with an eerie purpose.

IN THE ROAD

I had a dream last night, I dreamt
I was trying to shoe a horse in the road.
I'd get under him and swing my hammer
and he'd move his foot, just a little. Hitting
the nails was like trying to strike flies
from the air. My hammer flashed in the sun,
striking the shoe to the left or the right of the nail.
One miss-hit busted my thumb open.
Blood trickled like a wet glove over my hand.
I cursed as he hopped around on three legs,
a totally blank expression on his face.
Occasionally a car came down the road, slowly,
carving a wide arc around us, the passengers
with their windows rolled up, looking silently
out at me, sometimes shaking their heads.
I'd swing and miss. Then swing and hit my thumb.
Finally I swung, he shifted his foot, and my hammer
hit my kneecap with some amazing velocity.
I crumpled to the ground like a worn-out flag.
This horse just stood there, expressionless.
Another car passed by, very close to me.

A child in the backseat cracked her window a bit.
She held out a banana and pretended to shoot me
in the head. She silently mouthed the word *pop*
twice—*pop, pop*—and I felt myself twitch sharply
in my bed. I knew I could wake up if I wanted to,
but it just wasn't my style.

BEAR PHOTO ·

Taken in Livingston, Montana
sometime around 1900,
this bear stands up perfectly straight
on hind legs, with his paws
together, up over his head
like maybe he's clapping,
like maybe he's praying
or pretending to pray,
really hamming it up,
but I'd say probably praying,
probably praying directly to God.
Yes, praying hard, directly to God.
It is a sunny day.

The photo is grainy.
The bear is shuffling about in the dirt street.
Dragging his hundred-pound chain.
Squinting into the sun.
Acting quite naturally.
Totally clueless as to how a man might pray.

THE PLANE

1

When someone feels they know you well enough
they might bear your children.
I was thinking about this when the plane took off.

2

The girl next to me is Russian.
Stewardesses aren't stupid.
It stinks in here like anchovy vinaigrette.

3

The plane's wing looks like a stage prop,
like a pretend wing, like a child's idea
of a wing.

4

When stripped to your socks,
all your coins in the tub,
you are moments away from being a terrorist.

5

The stewardess took from a passenger
a sugared walnut, and ate it.
The passenger had a bread sack full of them.

6

I'm looking out the window at the wing again.
It's like looking into someone's
girlfriend's ear, as she's sleeping.

7

I'm sound asleep when they come through
with the drinks. Dreaming
I'm having drinks on this airplane.

8

Grown men who carry sugared walnuts.
Grown men who offer walnuts
on airplanes.

9

The back of the plane smells.
What kind of work does
the word *smells* do?

10

The man in 13C says "ballsy"
twice in five minutes. Over
the wing's edge, the snow-dusted mountains.

11

I do a lot of listening.
I am a good listener.
I am entering a shrinking violet phase.

12

When people use the word *ballsy*
it always makes me smile. Far off
below, the snow-dusted mountains.

POEM

A book about a monk who
took care of encephalitic kittens,
a best seller.

I am standing here in the kitchen, alone.
It's 11 a.m. and I have my credit card in
my left hand. I've just bought
160 dollars' worth of steak
from a traveling salesman named Don.

Things have changed with me.
I no longer think it's fair
that retarded people can take the word
and have it all to themselves.

I turn the pages, looking at the pictures.

Obscenities as postulates, it's
what I've always said. Packets of energy,
discrete and separate,

things that come to me
as a kind of croissant pride.

The kittens, it seems, weren't making it.
I turn the pages.

The monk stood and—
fatuous! you would hiss—
let the Baltic Sea
lap gently at his feet.

IT

Little black ants are invading our bathroom.
They're coming in through a hole in our tile.
Tonight I look at one walking all over my floss case.
I have trouble crushing the ants.
But if I inadvertently flick one into the sink
and stare up at a spot on the wall
I seem to have no trouble flipping the faucet on,
full blast, and hosing him down the drain.
Grandma says I should write "it"—should hose "it"
down the drain. "Him," Grandma says,
"is too . . ." and she pauses . . .
I'm on the phone with my grandma.
She has no idea what the fuck she is saying.

They say one of the hardest things
for the young monks to master is
tennis.

I close my eyes and see a very large man
with a bright orange vest and hard hat.

When a young monk is battling distraction
they send him down the mountain
to take tennis lessons from the heathens.

The large man is yelling down
into an open manhole in
the middle of 42nd St.
Something about Gustav Mahler.

It's convincing, the young monk in the rain
with his wire basket of new balls.

"Mahler had visions, Douglas!
Hallucinations, Douglas!"

The new balls smell like Magic Markers.

Grandma is still making her point.
This is what I like about her.
Her voice comes somberly through the little grate
in my cell phone.

AT THE ACUPUNCTURIST'S

I was laid out like a mummy on the table.
It was my third or fourth time.
What don't you understand about *take
your socks off* she mumbled.
I tried to see my socks without lifting my head.

Have you been taking your Chinese herbs?
Yes.
All of them?
Yes.

A small bird hit the glass window;
it made a sharp thud.

I asked her, what's the most needles
you've ever put in someone?
She wouldn't say.
Fifty? I said.
She wouldn't say.
Seventy?
She pretended to be selecting the next needle.

If I strained I could just make out,
in my peripheral vision,
a wax ear over on the counter.
It was loaded up with needles.

II

Boss paused, said, "the ruthlessness
of lemongrass," noting the anger
in their autographs. Embrocations
of the madmen. Weather for feelings.
We translated for days in the wet tent.
Did they mean "mouth" of the river?
Pet Monkey's face was wrinkled.
We fed him.

*

Crystal learned to perform
some tasks, such as using
a key to unlock a door, then
opening the door, in only a week.
Other operations, such as removing
a record from its jacket and
putting it on a turntable, took
longer to master.

*

Fat? Maybe.

A grape candy melts on my tongue.

The gangrels samba through the sacristy.

I have this ferocious feeling.

The glacier scoots in an inch.

An ivory beak stabs sharply at my dream.

Varieties of corn rain down,

violating the autumn.

*

He said she was like a gorge to him.

How so? she said.

He didn't say. She said something

to rhyme with *meconium* and

turned, and walked away.

He had a Pernod on the coaster before him.

The seals indeed were in the harbor,

floating queerly like rockets.

*

It turns out God *does* play dice, poor
Einstein. He suffered "an orgy of
freethinking" at age twelve; enjoyed
a quiet sail on a European lake.
"Something deeply hidden had to be
behind things," he later said.
He sat hunched over at his desk.
He wore a cheap tan trench coat.

*

She cracked open the back door
and poked me out into the night,
just as one cracks open the window
of a passing sedan and pokes out
a wrapper, which I have described elsewhere.
The wind came through my sweater.
The night was a dazzling opponent.
The sky spat lightly all over me.

*

The warehouse was full of heads.
Indomitable dark clouds and
the pink of a theater, jiggle
of jodhpurs. Removing and lifting
was what the crafts were up to.
Not all the heads were human.
A carnival had been passing.
The birds sang. The gunwales: lavender.

*

They called him The Parvenu. Still
he was gracious. There were brief
chats with a sex gland. A rabbit slept
beside a construction site.
Stretched out in the soft dirt, his
feet like drugstore lucky rabbit feet.
One after another
orange pages settled the antiquary.

*

When I look at the box of Twinkies
they make me want to puke.
I eat ten of them.
Ten is all I can eat.
Now two remain, and I look at them.
For some reason I don't feel so sick.
I don't feel sick at all.
I think I can eat them.

*

You say you see me as "propped up,"
the way a leprechaun props himself
amid the moss and rocks at the river's edge.
Jill, to be fair, sat on Jack. On his face.
Later: auburn colloquies. A pulsing muscle
of birds. (*focus…focus…*) You,
you look into your soup but see deeply
into the trees, to the insides of spring.

*

*Couvade Makes a Comeback Amongst
the Religious Right,* reads the headline.
The gamecock tips back his rusty head
and lets out a throaty cackle.
At the town meeting the town dandy
insists we call him a fop. Insipid vagaries
bounce gently like echoes. "Coup de théâtre"
says the fop, frowning at the sound of it.

*

Large sign at edge of town reads
NATURAL TOYS, CLOTH DIAPERS.
A percolator runs amok, bubbles
over. News of a newborn named Omen.
Dusk. A tiny Italian waiter
kicks your shoe, says only
"flambé, tableside." An empty cup
vibrates slightly on its saucer.

*

I never tire of the inanities
& might get beat up tonight.
Shouldn't look at Tony's sister.
Etc.
A German sense of order over-
tightens the corset. And then there's
you, and Ray, looking down your noses
at my chardonnay.

*

The innervated spatula, it
feels things even you don't.
In 204 a couple humps briskly
like Great Danes, it's textbook (had heard
what was probably a shoe hit the wall
with some force). We dream of perfecting life
somewhere else. In space, let's say.
Wearing Erik Satie stretch pants.

*

The suicidal peahen stepped
out onto the busy interstate.
Rust on the metronome. One
dreadful entrechat after
another. The mezzo-sopranos
accused one another of straining.
You popped a gut, Del.
No you popped a gut, Bob.

*

An old British bicycle the color of
root beer. Missing children
buried in the autumn leaves.
An exciting new line of rustic
cowboy furniture called
Imperturbability. The first-term mayor
pedals confidently through town
with an ice cream.

*

A chilled aperitif slides toward me quickly
down the counter. We'd found the groom
in the sandbox without his cummerbund.
Holiday lights blinking on around town.
I knew at that moment that (1) I could never
be trusted; (2) my mind had softened some;
and (3) people were talking. Strange delays
in every wink and windfall.

*

A miniature dachshund named Herbert walks
backward up the gangplank. Rod swaps
sound-of-one-hand-clapping ringtone
for *portentous-late-night-motel-bedsprings.*
The sad, sad eyes of the local politician.
I loathe speculating but still sit around and
speculate. Endlessly. An autumn leaf disguised
as a large insect skitters out, across the wet patio.

*

More indeclinable adjectives, and a rhapsode
in the Porta-John. According to Jorge a bird
had made its nest on his breast. No sign
of life and so the nephews pulled
the wig from it. *Bravery ... Quietism ...*
Slide the pizza to one side—this reveals
a lacuna. It's where we thought the
table was. And can't be looked at long.

*

A note about pretzels fills this space.
Worry regarding the wind creates
a rip in the awning. Never again the
gelato al limone. An empty pair of
patent leather riding boots
stand menacingly in the doorway.
Chimps run chainsaws in my dreams.
If I can just take another minute of your time . . .

III

YARD WORK

4 JUNE 2009

Have been in yard.
Grass bits on face and glasses.
Weed whacking make me talk short.
Like robot on coffee break.
Like football coach at Sunday picnic.
"Dottie you sure look pretty tonight."
"Dottie you look real nice."
"Lorna this your potato salad?"
Have opened fridge door.
Am staring into fridge.
Have weed whacked long time.
Buzzing in hands and head.
Numbness in hands.
Smell of gasoline on sleeves.
Paper reads David Carradine
found quietly hanging
in hotel room closet
(I pause here)
from curtain cords

tied round neck and genitals . . .
(again, pause)
a final hard-on asserting itself, without question . . .
the apogee of decadence and boredom.

I lean on counter.
Am examining newspaper.
Am trying to feel something.
Anything.
He who conquers himself is the greatest warrior.
Yard looking good.
Memories of Lorna.
Hands numb. Real numb.
Can't feel thumbs.
Me weed whack long time.
Am looking at paper.
Am wanting to understand.
"Dottie you sure look pretty tonight."
And the hand above the marionette
casts a twitching shadow on the wall.
This always terrifies the children.

THE MOTORIST

I'm in the to-be-passed lane sipping a yerba maté, steering with my knee, trying to open a package of laxatives, checking cell calls, when past me glides a Lincoln

driven by a lady in pink sweats who sits like a turtle hunched at her wheel. Behind her, in the backseat, rides a mannequin, seat-belted in, well dressed (jacket & tie) except that his face has been peeled away or torn abruptly off.

His head vibrates like a lightbulb filament. There's a red, wet smear where his face was. I can just quickly glimpse this as I'm passed.

I'm listening to the news on the radio. The radio brings me the news of the day. We live in a very solid country.

GAMES IN THE SAND

As a boy I was taught not
to gobble my chocolates.
I had just learned to walk
and I'd play a game in the sand
with the other children.
I would stand there with my stick
and draw an animal from memory.
A cougar. A vole.

I'd draw an animal from memory
and ask them to guess.
If they guessed wrong
something terrible would happen
that week to someone in their family.

And then there's you.
When you were young you'd lay about
on a huge silk cushion
pulling the wings off hornets,
careful not to disturb them
in any other manner.
We were made for each other.

You, you gobbled your chocolates,
but we worked on that.
Now those days are behind us.

And you say, "huffing gas again."
And I can't keep from smiling a little.
As tourniquets of light cut across our field of vision.
And childhood memories flash like swans.
And we run down the gazelles just by thinking it.
And it's still like being little, really.

LEMON ICE CREAM

I am lying in my hotel bed,
facedown on the mattress again,
arms at my sides,
a slight breeze coming in through the window.

Earlier when I was up
I had looked for a long time
at the photo of a Baghdad man
on the dump (March '07 *New Yorker*).

He, too, facedown.
He wore a mint green oxford, pressed khakis,
dress socks (the shoes were missing).
His hands were tied behind his back with
what might have been phone cord.

But I am visiting this marvelous city
and can hear, through the open window,
the hot dog vendors arguing
across their polished carts.

*

Later in the park,
lemon ice cream of the highest quality.

And at the museum Braque's perfectly round *Soda*
about the size of a large pizza.

Cézanne's *The Smoker* went for 22,000 francs in 1909.

A pervading doom radiates
off a row of Otto Dixes.

An Émile Bernard that hung for decades
in a boardinghouse dining hall in Pont-Aven
("target of numerous breadballs").

A large, colorful Picabia—*Take Me There.*

Toulouse-Lautrec, Rousseau, Picasso—
(I'm walking, walking—)
a tiny Juan Gris—
Cornell and his feelings for the starlet—
a Kurt Schwitters fuming in the corner.

The word *soda* engages the mind.
Finally a Paul Klee etching makes me stop:
Two Men Meet, Each Believing the Other to Be of Higher Rank.
I stand there and look carefully at this.

Not far from me different men with their girlfriends
come and stand before the Rothko,
enthusiastically chopping at the air with their hands.

It is time to leave.

*

A second ice cream is allowed.
The pleasant chaos of a crowded park.
The sound of dozens of children shrieking.
Statues that make you feel like a visitor to Earth.

One statue in particular makes me feel like a mime.
A professional mime. But not a successful one.
One of the lesser mimes.

And so it is that my time in this city comes quietly to a close.

ANOTHER BANNER

We felt the robin was completely innocent.
I watched as the town drunk picked up his concertina.
A flea was singing its heart out on the veterinarian's wristwatch.

A limp mannequin was being blown
down the street, end over end
on his way to probably the river.
This we assumed was where he'd get in
and leave this town, facedown in the water.
He had no clothes on.
We watched him pass from within the warm Waffle House.

I'd risen early and gone outside to stare at the sky.
Me, a kind of king of bathos.
My wife watched me from the kitchen window.
She stood at the sink and leaned forward
and covered her face with her hands.
It was a gesture the gods were familiar with.

One banner read, THIS IS NOT A TIME FOR FEELINGS.
Another:

(the banner had nothing on it).

They hanged the robin at sundown.

I felt like a man in a park, dripping wet with gasoline.

Like a man with a tennis ball stuffed and taped into his mouth.

I tried to make a few sketches to express this,

pushing the tip of my pencil erratically up, down, up,

down, up . . . steadily across a blank sheet of paper.

What's wrong with this one? asked the doctor, later, adjusting my
    I V bottle.

I stared at a water stain on the ceiling.

Writer's block, said the nurse.

NOTES TO SELF

In the red-hot coals of the campfire I see the gently shifting face of a benevolent gorilla.

*

When you reach Enlightenment you just laugh. Right?

*

The somber way that motorcyclists wave to one another on the freeway.

*

Carol is on the porch. She lights a small cigar. It is dead calm out.

*

As I approached the spatula, everything Mom ever told me about them came rushing back.

*

Went to the park at 3 a.m. to look at the tennis courts. They were wet.

*

The old dog softly whines on his cushion.

*

When shirtless, men with long hair walk a certain way. They have to.

*

The last thing I remember was getting down on my hands and knees to watch the gumball go spiraling round and round on its way down the machine's clear plastic column.

*

Little puffs of air let loose from a campaign balloon.

*

Flyspecks on my eyeglasses keep me constantly paranoid.

*

Ataxia amid the daffodils.

*

Something mysterious and powerful about a tennis court at night.

*

The dead fly comes back to life on the quilt (begins wiggling legs).

*

Wet Ones, bear spray, Bible, rain hat.
Beer, saw, Milk Duds, matches.

*

The withdrawn sound of the Wiffle bat as it moves through the air.

*

Officers nap. The afternoon is bronze.

*

Use a conventional tone when talking to the mailman.

*

Never listen to Wagner while undressing.

*

Eat lunch like you mean it.

PEACE

A man has had surgery,
has splurged on some calf implants.
It is spring. The bluebirds are back.
Doctors put a white paper beak on the man's nose.
It will help him heal properly, they say.
People will stare at this beak instead of his calves, they say.
This will let him golf in peace, they say.
And peace is what he needs, they say.

WINDSOR

I wish now to speak plainly about a one-eyed horse I know.
His name is Windsor.

But first, parts of the horse:
mouth; nose; nostril;
face; forehead; forelock;
ear; poll; mane;
withers; ribs; flank;
loin; haunch; croup;
tail; thigh; buttock;
fetlocks; hooves; coronets;
pasterns; cannons; hock;
gaskin; stifle; belly;
knee; forearm; elbow;
shoulder; breast; neck;
throatlatch; lower jaw; cheek.

Windsor is old.
Where his left eye should be
there is a deep indentation.
It is completely furred over.
There looks to be some hay dust in there.

It is my job to trim Windsor's feet.
I am alone today.
His owner is in Cleveland.
Catching Windsor is no problem.
It requires simply walking up to him.

I tie Windsor to the fence.
I buckle my leather apron around my waist.
Windsor's left side is his evil side.
The right side is bright, optimistic,
perhaps a little nervous.
The left side is unsettling.
The left side gallops directly at one
like a cello solo. And so I duck
quickly back and forth beneath
his tied rope (horsemen: never do this)
and I note the evil Windsor, the bright Windsor,
the evil Windsor, the bright Windsor,
the evil Windsor, the bright Windsor,
back and forth and back and forth . . .
(my hat has fallen from my head).

Windsor, to be fair, doesn't move.
He stands there, and with one eye
stares out across the corral,
across Gallatin County, really,
looking into space I suppose

like one of our best philosophers
or mathematicians.

Occasionally a fly alights on him and his rump twitches.
But basically Windsor is motionless.
He is exploding with possibilities.

CHRISTMAS

A man falls in a parking lot, he
has been out Christmas shopping.
His eye is right down there,
down there against the asphalt.
When he opens his eye he sees a crack.
A regular thin crack in the asphalt.
Cars go around him. He won't get up.
For it is Christmas.

He looks directly into this crack.
He does not shy away.
What he sees there even a poet could not pretend to translate.

The edges of the crack bend his eyelashes a bit.
It is cold out and the various shoppers
drive left and right, around him.

A POSITION TO WITNESS

When one is old one can step into a cemetery
and feel like Joseph's donkey, and take little steps,
and trip.

One can go through the cemetery during a snowstorm
and brush off all the tombstones
and straighten all the pots of dead or plastic flowers
and get cold, and look around, and lie down and die.

But let's not get carried away.
For now let's focus on stepping into a cemetery
and tripping, and moving like a donkey.
A biblical donkey.

The best biblical donkeys are always
staggering through crowded marketplaces
and knocking booths over, trampling farm stands,
pulling wagons onto their sides. They get to look
into moonlit wells at three in the morning.
They get to see prophets and the young wives of warriors
making toast completely naked. They are privy

to all sorts of conspiracies and bent governments.
People lay bare their innermost aspirations
to these donkeys, and these donkeys soak it up.
They are in a position to witness.
This is a distinguishing characteristic.
This is what sets the biblical donkey apart.

Which is why you shouldn't feel bad about stepping
into a desolate cemetery, feeling like a shit-caked donkey.
You should step in and stumble. Trot some if you can.
Crack marble crosses off. Slobber into a sparkling cistern.
Paw a gash in the ground. And with your mental eye
travel up and over the Pleiades, looking down on D.C.,
Sam's Club, the Sea of Cortez,
bustling Nineveh, parts of Poland, and Billings.

ADVICE FOR THE POET

Never aim your bicycle at a chicken.
Never set your glasses on an anvil.

HUMANS

Humans learn early to smile to keep from being eaten. Also to aid in procreation. Those are the only reasons. Clear writing is clear thinking. Run your finger down your verbal blintz. Here comes the indecorous cube steak. Crawdads, like lobsters with feelings. A freshly painted fingernail tapping the counter at the courthouse.

They put a heavy machine on my head. It felt and smelled like an old manual typewriter. "To better study the human skull," they said. Raising the usual questions of *Character*, of *Capacity*. (Could not stop licking my lips.) Of *Sublimity, Ideality, Mirth, Time.*

POEM

The nitwit danced with the congresswoman
at the spring picnic.

I went down to the river to take a good look at it.
I stood on the bank and said "God, if you do exist—"

A handsome puppet passed, dragging its puppeteer by the hand.

Also a Pekingese wearing a University of Mobile sweatshirt.

To those people who are always talking about "surrealism"
can I suggest opening your fucking eyes?

If you do this, you will see mothballs. And a green nightgown.

DIANA

A sudden aching tenderness filled Diana's heart.

"I suppose you think I should be supremely happy."

He was a large man. Heavyset. He made her think of Mussolini.

She hesitated, looking adorably wistful and pathetic.

"Don't worry. Wild horses couldn't make me invite a girl to dinner, unless I wanted to," said Arthur.

Diana was not listening.

She was reliving those few moments in Seton's studio.

Almost sheepishly Arthur drew a box from his pocket.

Diana had not imagined his opinions could wound so deeply.

She was to look back on those hours with tears of longing.

A wrinkle appeared between Elizabeth's eyes.

"No nice girl likes to be pawed."

She was in her bedroom, but the door was open.

Stanton came, fortified by chocolates.

The conversation remained mostly between men.

Vivian looked puzzled.

"Well, what's this thing about being yourself again?"

The furniture was a collection of surprisingly beautiful antiques.

Diana felt as if she were sinking into a scented, silken sea.

A man was there. One of the most distinguished-looking men

she had ever seen. With a face hard as nails,

iron-jawed, powerful, and exquisite manners.

"Oh, have you lived in New York City?"

Diana ran down the stairs gratefully.

She was sure a heart of gold must beat beneath that ugly sweater.

Beachy began a whispered conversation with her "Charles."

She would never forget her pantomime of a starving artist.

Then Mrs. Burton purred, "I see you've had a letter from your husband."

Beachy sat down beside her.

Some time ago Diana had noticed that Beachy

was not so naughty anymore.

The next day she spoke to Mr. Klesalek about it.

"Well?" prodded the unquenchable one.

Beachy thumped the pillows behind her bobbed head.

The nurse smiled and left the room.

Diana could not trust herself to reply.

Tears of gratitude welled in Elizabeth's eyes.

Dr. Wayne returned at 10 o'clock.

He frowned as he took Paul's blood pressure.

Diana pondered, feeling the need of immediate rest.

She must have walked blocks before it occurred to her to take a car.

Wet-eyed, she "lightly and ironically" portrayed the countess.

Shepherd Seton put his hands behind his back and said patiently,

"Go on, I deserve it."

Go on? The idea sickened Diana.

Arthur was frankly pleased with her.

She dressed carefully that evening.

Instantly the look she dreaded leaped into Elizabeth's eyes.

Arthur's voice was not so pleasant.

After that it became their weekly custom to plan something.

Bob and Ben had stopped on the way out for a drink at the bar, but Arthur did not join them.

Diana imagined Stanton's refusal irritated Arthur.

He smiled. A poker smile.

She stared at him innocently.

Diana's lips were trembling.

There was a smell of burning meat.

Stanton spoke up: "I thought Mrs. Vane might enjoy seeing my studio."

Diana pictured herself stepping from peak to peak of artistic accomplishment.

"I'm beautiful," she cried softly.

It gave her all the comfort of a familiar glance.

Vivian asked about Diana's work. "I wonder," continued Vivian, "what name you intend to use." It ended with laughter.

"Men are nothing in my life," Diana retorted glibly.

The class smiled. But now tears were rolling down her cheeks.

Klesalek's tone changed.

Vivian flung away from her and began to pace the floor.

"Damn!" exploded Vivian. Her voice was bitter.

Her face was flushed and as sweet as wet apple blossoms.

"You little fool. You precious baby idiot!"

Absorbed in her thoughts, she did not see Arthur crossing the street.

Not until he had lifted his hat.

"You don't miss a thing, do you?"

"Not a melancholy signal like that. Have I been talking too much?"

Her utter lack of self-consciousness pleased him.

Diana had the uneasy sensation of having waded in beyond her
    depth.

Older people are more apt to take things to heart.

Arthur smiled appreciatively, but with a new expression.

There appeared now a new Diana, inherently domestic.

Stanton took his chocolates and left.

Vivian seemed nervous.

"Take off your things, dear, and have some tea.

Mr. Winterble is just going."

The next day was Saturday, and Diana decided to discipline herself

by calling on Mrs. Burton. As she entered Nadine's car

she was surprised at the richness of its dark upholstering.

Mrs. Burton rose. Mrs. Burton snapped her darning cotton

and gave them a caustic glance.

She realized she was beautiful yet didn't understand

the heady quality of her deep blue eyes.

Never so long as she lived would Diana forget the scene that
    followed.

"Telephone, dear!"

Morning found her weak and listless.

Diana had no business letting him touch her.

"That's a long time," she had said. "Yes," he had said.

Then: "The end is really a game called the survival of the fittest."

Vivian said flatly, "Arthur Vane is not the kind of man . . ." (she
    trailed off meekly).

Diana faltered: "I'm going to have a career," she said,

feeling the need of immediate rest.

She dropped her clothes on the floor, wrapped a thin kimono

about her aching body and threw herself

on the bed. "Paul!" she called.

There was no answer. By morning she supposed

she'd be saying she had no idea the pistol was loaded.

Vivian rose, fastening her coat with trembling fingers.

We might call Mr. Klesalek, she said.

Beachy then spoke: "We are going to be very circumspect, Diana."

She threw back her coat and sipped her tea.

Diana made a delicately browned ragout

(Arthur pushed it aside)

and went to her room to finish packing.

Presently there came the sound of Nadine's voice.

Not strong but very sweet and clear.

"He makes the wildest love," she admitted frankly.

"Never mind, dear," Diana comforted her.

Round and round like a squirrel in a cage went Diana's thoughts.

The violent ringing of the doorbell roused her.

"Vivienne what?"

"Just Vivienne. She is very well known in artistic circles."

Diana was twisting her handkerchief into a succession of knots.

Instantly the look she dreaded leaped into Elizabeth's eyes.

When she returned to the library, Marion and Louis were conversing,

rather self-consciously. Marion rose and flounced out,

closing the door. "I'm tottering on the verge of forty."

Arthur put Diana into a taxi. He said, "Thank you

for a delightful evening." Until that moment Diana

had felt no necessity for PLANS.

"Oh Arthur," she gulped. "You win."

She returned home to sit with a book in her hands,

but without turning a page.

AFTER A TERRIFYING NAP

Gratitude came down
in the form of a golden
grasshopper.

Not golden like a bar of gold
(an ingot)
or golden like honey
or paint on a football helmet.
It was another kind of gold.

This grasshopper
glanced in through the open
window of a southbound car,
hit the fleeced shoulder of
a sleeping infant and bounced
down onto the floor.
It came to rest beside a potato chip.

The grasshopper sent forth a golden light.
The infant awoke in his car seat,

looked at the grasshopper
and wiggled his feet, his white socks.

It is likely we are completely ignorant
of our role in the universe.

WHAT CAN WE LEARN FROM POETRY?

Walken was angry but stoic last night
(*Communion*, 1989, color, 103 min.)
when it came time to take his anal probe.
The little blue doctors were brisk
but not excessive.

The whole thing made me look
more hopefully upon the future,
realizing the desire to "talk
things over" is human, but
also sometimes futile.

(Quite a lot of time passes here where the poet puts his head down,
where the poet no longer has his head up.)

And now Richard Gere with
the gerbils . . . it's all
coming back to me . . .

Thinking quickly of another poet, John Barr.
They say, affectionately, I think, that
he is a "small, sun-baked man."

*

Definitely more stoic than angry, when it came time.
It somehow touched me.

This morning the neighbors, resituating their sprinklers.
A wet cricket crawls out into a patch of sunlight.

The downtown walks have been hosed.
Outside the bank some hanging plants drip.
A group of senior citizens enters a café, so I follow.

Inside, pancakes lie docilely.
I see a comb-over blown loose.
The bravado of croissants.
Says the one with Peter Lorre eyes:
"Don't bring my grape juice
in a glass boot."

*

Again, rent *Communion*.
They say we're fucked.
My plaid fedora says *HECHO EN CHINA*.
Our president purses his lips
like an aggrandized dachshund.

Sitting around praying for miracles
is like dying a slow death screams
the life coach, spitting into
the front row.

At any rate, I saw an octogenarian
in town today. I stopped.
I helped her eat her pancake.

THE NEIGHBOR

The neighbor said, "But seriously, who is it you're writing these for? Surely you have an audience in mind." I thought about it carefully, I did, but ended up repeating almost word for word what I had already said, which was that the poems were written for me, or for readers who were exactly the same person I was. I said I couldn't imagine any other person. I said I could see how that probably sounded disingenuous, or solipsistic, or both. And just then a small dinner roll fell from the table, rolled across the living room steadily, not slowing at all, or wobbling. It rolled across the room and passed through the doorway into the bedroom and the door slammed shut behind it.

A BOLD COAT OF VODKA BONBONS

It started out simply enough. I wanted to paint the guest bedroom.
I went to the paint store to get a gallon of Chewy Caramel.
I'd seen it in *Men's Journal.*

"Yes," said the clerk, "and you'll want a quart of Nutmeg Frost for
    the trim."
"All right then," I said, and I turned to leave but the clerk spun me
    around.
"And what if Chewy Caramel is too dark, too strong for the room?"
    he said.
"One can easily overpower a guest bedroom."

"Too strong?" I said. "The Chewy Caramel?"
"Yes," he said, and he dropped a gallon can of Lazy Bedouin
into my cart, followed by a quart of Ruined Crops.

"Okay," I said. "I see what you mean."
"Wait," he said, "don't go,"
and he dropped in a gallon of Curb Water,
along with a quart of Idiot Savant.

"And take this just in case," he said, and he dumped in a gallon
of Caesar Salad, as well as a quart of Wartime Marigold.
"Thank you," I said, looking at him.

The clerk was gripping my coatsleeve. I shook him loose
and backed away a bit with my loaded cart.
He was holding something—another can of paint—in his hand.
I tried to turn my cart quickly but the clerk was able to forcefully toss
one last can into the cart: a quart of Lavender Eyes.
"You might need it," he shouted, as I ran with my cart to the register.

Once home I began painting the guest bedroom.
I started with the Chewy Caramel but something wasn't right.
Was it too dark or not dark enough? I was about to pop open the can
of Lazy Bedouin when my wife walked in.

She said she'd been out running errands—she
had picked up some paint for the guest bedroom.
She looked at my pants and shirt covered with Chewy Caramel.
"Stop," she said, "we won't need your paint."

Before I knew it my wife was painting over the Chewy Caramel
with a bold coat of Vodka Bonbons.
Her hand moved like a butterfly across the wall.
"Open the Bay of Pigs," she chirped, not looking at me.
And then, before I could move: "No, Baby Finger!
I need to see the Baby Finger!"

UPON OUR RETURN

When we walk into the room
(it is late)
the child is there on the floor,
working on the Harry Truman puzzle.

HELLO

The man in the porno is lying back on the plastic lounge chair.

His eyes seem loose in his head.

Like maybe they don't belong to him.

They flutter like the delicately hinged eyes of a doll

surfacing from a parallel universe.

I hit Pause.

These eyes are trying to tell us something.

They are trying to help us.

Anyone who looks into them can easily see this.

It is difficult to understand how the world works.

(The paused screen vibrates, almost imperceptibly.)

Take this morning, for example—a man removed his shoes

and threw them at our president.

Directly at our president's head.

One shoe after another.

Lately our president's smirks have grown noticeably fainter.

When recounting this shoe incident to reporters

our president said it was "weird."

And, "I don't know what his beef is."
The paused screen vibrates, almost imperceptibly.
The doll surfaces so quietly.
A slight static in the air.

THE MAN

He got tired of his body.
That's what the papers said.
And that he jumped from a bridge.
And when you turned to page 4
that's all it said again,
in the plainest typeface,
he got tired of his body.

Sometimes I put a taco into my body,
or I walk slowly through the dark bedroom
(I have to take a leak)
like a head with legs,
like a marionette with my arms out,
wondering where the dresser is, or,
where is the monster jade plant?
My feet shuffle slowly across
the rough pine floor like
the feet of a cross-eyed circus bear—
up! up! (he's on his hind legs)—
who wants only his blue tambourine,
which raises some really good questions.

A fisherman looked up and saw the man jump.
He said, "I looked up and saw the man jump."
He said that the man flapped his arms,
that the man had definitely changed his mind,
that it was a nice day, and that the man
was trying to fly over to a tree.

CITY AT NIGHT

I was at the acupuncturist's.
Me again, I said to the ceiling.

I'd been put in the Crucifix Room.
This was a room where the walls
and ceiling were lined with
crucifixes. Every square inch.
Crucifixes of all sizes; of wood, metal,
and polished bone; of colored glass and jewels.
It was like being inside a giant helmet.
A kind of helmet of crucifixes.

She had put the needles in
and left me in the dark.
A single candle flickered on the desk.
I felt my lower lip sagging a bit.
I lay there breathing.
I was like a city at night.

Beside me flowed a river.
I was a city at night on the banks of a river.

The various crucifixes flashed a little
in the moonlight, sound of water lapping.
There were a thousand struggling souls in that city.
Usually they'd be crying out to God.
But this particular night they quietly let
the blue light go coursing through the parks,
past auto dealerships, past bakeries,
through hospital courtyards, down the long alleys,
through the train station and each of the train cars.

After a while God called down to them.
He hadn't heard from them.
It was all very strange to him.

NOTE AND ACKNOWLEDGMENTS

All lines in "Diana" were lifted from Vida Hurst's
1927 novel *Diana* (Grosset & Dunlap, New York),
with the exception of "Stanton took his chocolates
and left," which was added by the author.

The author gratefully acknowledges the following
magazines/journals, where many of these poems
originally appeared: *Bear Parade*; *The Believer*;
Calaveras; *Cirque*; *Forklift, Ohio*; *Fou*; *HoboEye*;
notnostrums; *Octopus*; *Sorry For Snake*;
Talking River Review; and *Washington Square*.

The author thanks everyone, in all departments,
at Wave Books for their meticulous work,
insights, patience and support.

The author also thanks Alex Phillips for
loaning him his baby finger (again).

Michael Earl Craig was born in Dayton, Ohio
in 1970. He earned degrees from the University
of Montana and the University of Massachusetts.
He is the author of *Can You Relax in My House*
(Fence Books, 2002) and *Yes, Master* (Fence
Books, 2006). He is a Certified Journeyman
Farrier and lives near Livingston, Montana,
where he shoes horses for a living.